Robyn's
LIFE JOURNEY

A Memoir of a Woman's Ongoing Journey
Toward Enlightenment

ROBYN FORD

BALBOA
PRESS
A DIVISION OF HAY HOUSE

ISBN: 978-1-4525-5659-8 (sc)
ISBN: 978-1-4525-5660-4 (e)

First Edition

Balboa Press books may be ordered through booksellers or by contacting:
Balboa Press
A Division of Hay House
1663 Liberty Drive
Bloomington, IN 47403
www.balboapress.com
1-(877) 407-4847

Cover Design Is Robyn's Latest Artwork Titled "Sun Kissed Tulips"

Printed in the United States of America

Balboa Press rev. date: 08/28/2012

To all the people who overcame their fear and found themselves.

Thanks to

My friend Gabriole without her help this book would not have been possible and to my son Jarod for his love and support.

Contents

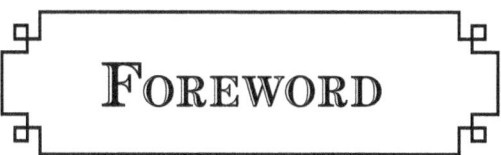

FOREWORD

MY DESIRE FOR THIS BOOK is that it will inspire readers to seek a spiritual life. I'm not a writer and have never had any great desire to be a story teller, but I've had a nagging need to write my autobiography. The feeling started many years ago when it was easy to dismiss because I still needed to live my life. It seems rather silly to write a memoir of a life half-lived. That has changed, not because I'm so terribly old, but because I've come through some major changes and it seemed reasonable to put things down on paper, if only to try and make sense of it for myself. In doing so, I can see patterns and how decisions have moved me forward. I always had choices and I'm very grateful for the choices that I made. I don't know what would have happened if I had done "y" instead of "z". Perhaps I'd learn the same lessons, just in a much slower or difficult process. Perhaps I'd learn nothing of any lasting value and could have just lived a life of pleasure – skimming on the surface of things. In any case, I am grateful for where I am today. That might seem odd once you read my story, but it is the truth. The lessons haven't always been easy ones, but they've certainly been lasting.

Many spiritual teachers are convinced that the karmic wheel is now broken. We are in such a new place and new time that we can truly be co-creators now. We still have to do the deep work of processing our ego. This means looking at the fears, habits and out-dated beliefs that run us. We need to look at these things very clear-eyed and let them go. If it isn't processed, we'll just drag it with us into the new era. The good news is that the processing can go much faster now because world consciousness is much lighter than it has been in hundreds of years.

As I said there are many ways to do this work. Find a path that resonates best for you.

PREFACE

I HAVE SPENT HALF MY life trying to figure out what the purpose of life on earth is. Some people spend most of their lives in this quest, and others don't give it a second thought. I feel very fortunate that the question started pestering me relatively early. Trying to find answers has made life much more interesting than it would have been. We have to be ready for the many paths that life will take us as we look for answers. We are taught not to ask questions and not to stray from accepted roles, so sometimes the answers have to bang us on the head pretty hard before we pay attention. My spiritual education came with a few knocks, but each time I picked myself up an amazing thing happened – I became stronger and stronger. This isn't a story of woe, far from it. I was extremely fortunate in being born into a comfortable home in Australia. It is a story of how our decisions can lead us to where we need to be, or away from it.

My childhood was a happy one, although I do recall at around age seven having very strange dreams of falling into an abyss. Now, on recalling it, my memory of falling into a body was a similar feeling when I landed on this earth. I feel that I do not belong here and agreed to make this journey and take on this life. Perhaps most of us feel this way and that is why we feel so alone and homesick without even knowing what or where we are homesick for.

The time has come to get things down on paper. There is so much more to whom we are than just the life we see here on earth. I am not from this earth but am part of it whilst I am here. We all have interesting stories to tell. This is mine.

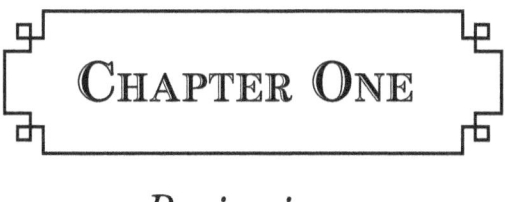

Beginnings

A Peaceful Childhood

I WAS BORN ROBYN FORD on February 24, 1944, an only child to my Australian parents. My father was a soldier and my mother was the daughter of a station master from the railways. We lived in a small country town on the southeast coast of New South Wales in Australia.

As a child I went to a Catholic school and was educated by nuns where I was taught to fear my sins. If I did not learn my catechism the nuns would give me a tap on my hands. I suppose that not learning the catechism was another sin to be feared, but it was actually the nuns that I feared.

They told me that if I received a calling to become a nun I must answer it so each week when I was in church I would pray to God saying, "Please do not call me." I don't think that was what the nuns intended.

When I was about eight or nine I went to confess my sins at church. The sin was missing Sunday mass a few times. The priest got so angry with me and made me feel so guilty that I never went back again. I guess you could say that his anger backfired. Why was it such a huge sin? Perhaps they worried that their indoctrination wouldn't take hold if I missed mass. There isn't one perfect religion. Loving our creator, or source is the way to find peace and love inside of us. This will give us the fulfillment we are all seeking.

This is not to say that I had terrible schooling. In general I have good memories of my school days. But I am grateful that I never felt the slightest pull to become a nun. In fact, upon graduation I was quite excited to begin the rest of my life.

New Guinea – Stepping into Adulthood

In 1962, when I was eighteen, my parents decided to go to New Guinea to manage coffee plantations in the highlands. From Sydney we flew in a propeller plane to Port Moresby, which is the main town on the east coast of New Guinea. We had to wait there for a few days before flying to Madang where my father had a few days of business to attend to. Once that was out of the way we were to make the final leg of the trip aboard the cargo plane that would fly us to the coffee plantation in the highlands.

My parents and I settled in to the Port Moresby hotel then went downstairs to the only good restaurant in town for dinner. My father was a very friendly sort and quickly began a conversation with two Canadian geologists sitting at a table beside us. They had just arrived from Canada and were on a working trip.

One of the geologists was a very handsome, tall Canadian, about twenty-four-years-old. The attraction was instant and mutual. For "some reason" we kept bumping into each other. Finally he invited me to see a movie with him when we were in Madang. The movie theatre was like no other that I had experienced. The roof was open and it was stinking hot, but that discomfort was a minor irritation because I was with someone very special. I have no idea what the movie was.

We liked each other a lot. Even though I was relatively inexperienced I knew that what I felt for him was a very deep connection. I was in love. He suggested that I go back with him to Canada. I was very tempted but was scared to leave my parents, after all, I was only eighteen and it was a different world back then. Young women didn't fly across the world after someone they just met. I gave him my address and he promised to write me. I wonder how my life would have changed had I made the decision to go with him. No doubt I was destined to live in Canada because the opportunity was presented to me again fourteen years later.

At the time, I had a boyfriend in Australia and when I returned to Sydney I broke off with him and told him that I had met a Canadian whilst away. He did not take this well and we had a huge argument. Since my Canadian geologist friend promised to write to me I waited for his letter to arrive. The weeks and months went by and no letter. I became very sad that it never came. I later realised that my Australian boyfriend had access to my parent's mailbox and collected our mail because he was in business with my father. Was it possible that he took the letter? I know that he was capable of doing so. He was not exactly an upstanding citizen. I later learned that he had actually forged my mother's signature on a cheque and cashed it.

I said my good-byes to my young Canadian geologist without realizing that I'd never see or hear from him again and joined my parents to continue our journey to the plantation. Whilst my parents and I were waiting for the cargo flight a group of native New Guineans arrived on the tarmac. They had just been to a celebration and were taking the flight home. They were wearing ostrich feathers in their hair with banana leaves tied around their waist and had rubbed pig oil on their bodies. The heat was almost unbearable and the smell of the pig oil did not make for a pleasant wait. Pigs were very important to them and in fact some of the women would help breastfeed the piglets if the sow couldn't or wouldn't feed it.

When the plane landed and took on its cargo the natives rushed to take their seats. My parents boarded with the natives and I decided to wait. This turned out to be a big mistake. As I boarded the plane I observed that it was hollow inside with the cargo tied in the middle of the plane with old rope. The seating was a long bench along either side of the aircraft. Because I was the last one on, I had to sit at the end of the bench and only had a small strap around my waist to hold me in place. The plane took off at a sharp upward angle and everyone fell downward toward me. I was pushed off my seat by the crush of sliding people and landed on the floor with the belt around my neck.

I heard a quiet laughter coming from the natives and realised why no one wanted to be the last one on. It was a good lesson for me to not take myself too seriously. Once I found my sense of humour and relaxed, I found New Guinea to be a fascinating country. Even today I still count it as one of the most interesting places I've ever visited.

Late that afternoon we arrived at the coffee plantation and I began my introduction to pidgin English. A young native named Asa gave me a gift. It was a comb that he had made especially for me from the wood of a local tree. I was told that it was a typical comb that they used for their hair. I turned it over to see some very interesting signs on it. On the back Asa carved in Pidgin English: "Asa me work him cowom." Translation: my name is Asa and I made this comb.

The natives had developed Pidgin English in order to communicate with the English-speaking plantation owners. There were many languages in New Guinea when the Europeans first arrived. I don't know how many of the languages survive today, but pidgin is still common.

I still have the comb today.

First and Last Date

My father suggested that it would be beneficial for me to go back to Australia and work in an advertising agency. He noticed that I had an artistic side. He researched several companies and finally decided on an old established one in downtown Sydney. I delivered my resume and was hired. It seemed that my career in advertising was launched, so I said good-bye to my parents who were to live in New Guinea for several more years while I began the next stage of my life.

I continued living in their home in Sydney while working in the advertising agency. My father was quite right about the agency, it did indeed bring out my creative side, but the real joy was being back in Sydney. It was an exciting city to be in at the time. There were many jazz bars and I would meet friends after work for drinks of sherry with a background of jazz making us all feel much more sophisticated than we were.

When I was twenty I met my husband. He had just arrived back in Australia from a years' vacation in Holland and landed a position at the agency where I was working. He and his parents had emigrated from Holland about twelve years prior.

After a few short weeks he advised his friends that if he dated me he would marry me. His friends laughed and bet him one-hundred dollars that there was no way that I would accept. At that time Australians stuck to their kind and were not likely to date Europeans.

I found him to be very different from anyone I'd previously dated and was definitely taken with this very handsome young man. He had a romantic and attentive personality which was so unlike the Aussie boys I knew. A short time later he did try to ask me out, but I declined as I already had a date. I felt bad about declining so I invited him to a party that I was giving for one of my friends and he accepted.

He was so nervous coming to the party that he drank a bit too much in order to get up the courage to propose. He asked me to dance and after a few minutes he said he wanted to marry me. I thought he was crazy and drunk, or just crazy drunk, but by the next day I was convinced that he was serious. I accepted his proposal and he won his bet. Drunk or not, it seems we were meant to be together as he knew the moment he saw me that I was the one for him.

My future husband was not Catholic and my parents were very upset about it. The local priest came to see me and told me that I would be committing a mortal sin by marrying outside of my faith. I was so determined to marry that I didn't listen. I guess the nuns didn't instill enough fear in me. I know now that there is nothing wrong in marrying someone outside of your religion, but I will admit that the priest did manage to burrow into my mind and sow some seeds of doubt. Somehow though, I was determined to go ahead with the marriage and see past the family's prejudice.

We were married three months after his proposal on September 5, 1964, in a registry office in Sydney, Australia. Our parents attended the ceremony, but they were clearly not very happy. There was some speculation that we "had" to get married, but our first child came along three years after the fact. We were simply in love and didn't see any reason to wait. After the ceremony we celebrated with about thirty friends at a local hotel.

When I looked at my astrology chart many years later I saw that our moon placements were both in Pisces at the time of our meeting. I was told that this indicated that we were destined to meet. It also showed that I bring wealth to the person I marry which did happen later in the marriage. We knew that whatever we had would be from our own work and not any handouts. In our early days we got by with such things as cushions on the floor in place of chairs and a cardboard box for our dining table.

Despite our ad-hoc furniture, he had big dreams and told me that by the time we were thirty we would be millionaires. His confidence appealed to me, besides we were young newlyweds and besotted with each other. It was quite a combination for a convent-educated twenty-year-old.

Back to New Guinea

After a few months of marriage I was missing my parents terribly and decided to visit them in New Guinea.

It was Father's Day when I arrived in Port Moresby and to my dismay no one was there to meet me. Had my father not received my telegram telling him of my arrival? How was I going to get into the highlands to Kinantu without his help? As I was asking for information at the terminal counter, two geologists overheard me and offered me a lift in their four-seater Cherokee plane since they also happened to be going to

Kinantu. I sat in the front next to the pilot and they sat in the back. My only concern now was how to get to my father's coffee plantation once we landed. I was looking at a four-hour drive up the mountains through very rough terrain and that was with the assumption that I would be able to find a car for hire. I was grateful that I was at least part-way there and I would face the challenge of the last leg when I arrived in Kinantu.

The plane took off at a ninety-degree angle as we needed to clear the huge mountain ahead of us. I was feeling grateful that I didn't have people and pigs sliding into me this time! About thirty minutes into the flight my door suddenly flew open and I could see the forest hundreds of feet below. As I began to panic the pilot simply leaned across in front of me, reached out, and closed the door. He told me that the pilots in New Guinea were very experienced as this was one of the roughest terrains in the world and not to worry. Apparently the door was not closed tightly enough when we left, he calmly told me. The pilot then proceeded to instruct me to keep my eyes open as I would see some crashed planes below from years back. This did not make me feel very safe; however we did arrive in one piece.

At the same time my father had decided to make the drive to the outpost to collect the mail just in case I had sent him a Father's Day card. He had no idea that I was on a flight to see him. My telegram was sitting at the post office waiting for pick-up. He was thrilled when he discovered that I was on my way and would be arriving soon. I was very relieved when I saw my parents waving to me as the plane landed. His timing was perfect, but part of me still wonders if it was his intuition that made him decide to make the long drive.

I spent two wonderful weeks with my parents at the coffee plantation. It was a fresh assignment for my father so I was excited to see the new place. It was huge and the tour of the grounds took several hours. His love for the place really came through as he showed me the coffee trees and the harvesting and drying process.

That first night I went to my parent's bedroom to say good night. I noticed that my father slept with a gun beside him. When I asked why he did that he replied that he needed the gun because sometimes the wild pigs would come onto the coffee plantation and damage the plants. I then went to my room and opened my window to smell the jungle before falling asleep. In the morning I accidently found out that the reason for the gun was not for the wild pigs, but for the cannibals that lived in the next valley. The very next night I closed my window tight because I did not want to be someone's dinner. Eventually I did relax and realized that the cannibalism might be slightly exaggerated – at least that was the thought that I clung to.

It was a good thing that I didn't know too much or I would've been too nervous to enjoy my time at the plantation. I came across a news piece in the online version of the Sydney Telegraph that made it very clear that cannibalism is still very much an ongoing issue in the region. "The cannibal cult is accused of killing and eating seven people – five men and two women. . . The police commander said several members had confessed to eating body parts and making soup from the victims." *The Telegraph*, July 13, 2012.

Luckily if anything like that was going on while I was there it was kept very quiet. I was able to relax and have a wonderful time with the locals. They were excited to meet me since I was the daughter of the plantation manager. They asked what I liked to eat and I replied that I loved corn. The next morning when I went outside, to my surprise, there was corn piled up three-feet high at the back door. Apparently the word went out to all the villages and they collected corn for me. I was surprised and grateful for their kindness, but I did get tired of eating corn. My parents ended up sharing it with the natives who worked on the plantation.

One interesting custom that I discovered in the Sepik area of New Guinea is that they greet each other by caressing each other's private parts as an acknowledgement. The men wear a penis gourd on their penis. Of course this sounds outrageous to us, but this is their custom and who are we to make judgement. Sometimes the older mothers also greet their sons with the same custom.

Of course the lovely visit had to end and I returned to married life in Australia.

Life is Simple Yet Complicated

By the time my husband and I reached thirty we had two children. We were living a middle-class life and were very comfortable. We owned our house and two cars but had not yet reached the promised millionaire status, so my husband stated that by forty we would become millionaires. He became even more focused and studied every book that he could find on how people became millionaires.

Our life was very happy one. I had stopped working at the advertising agency to take care of our children. My husband would go to work and I would spend many mornings on the beach with my children enjoying the sun and surf. We travelled to Fiji several times and spent a fabulous few weeks on a small island off the coast of Suva (one of the main coastal towns there). Fiji is a popular tourist destination for Australians as it is only a four-hour flight from Sydney.

This idyllic existence changed suddenly when my father died at the young age of fifty-two whilst having heart surgery. I was devastated and could not comprehend this sudden tragedy. My spiritual journey had not yet begun and I had thought that my father would always be with me. I felt that my life had fallen apart. I reacted very badly and even went so far as to blame everyone from the doctors to my mother for his death.

I now realise that reacting this way was hurting many people, including my deceased father. I was only thinking of myself and now know that the deceased person stays for up to nine days before moving into another layer. When someone holds onto a loved one it causes much anguish for the deceased and they suffer terribly because they see and hear everything and this action can hold them back from a smooth transition.

I know that this is not my real home here on earth. It often feels like a dream to me and one day when I leave this body I will wake up and see that it was all a learning experience. I worry that it would be a wasted life if I die before learning and achieving what I came here for: to find my path and achieve enlightenment. Perhaps this is why so many people fear death. Deep, deep down they know that they haven't done what they came here to do. My feeling is that if we achieve our purpose in life we will not be afraid to die.

Just imagine that creation is a vast ocean and we are tiny drops of water in it. When we take on a body from this ocean we begin a life. But we are always connected to the ocean, even when we are immersed in our three-dimensional lives on earth. When our life here is finished we simply go back into the ocean, i.e., source. It can be difficult to remember that we are not the ego, we are source and that really is the whole point of awakening – to remember who we really are.

Imagine also that our body is a glove and we are the energy in this glove so if we take off the glove it is not able to move. It needs us to move it. It also needs us to energise it with nourishment so we need to respect it in order to obtain maximum benefit from it.

CHAPTER TWO

Moving to America

Who Wants to Be a Millionaire?

MY HUSBAND DECIDED THAT WE weren't going to make our millions in Australia by the time we reached thirty and suggested that we relocate to America. I agreed to the move. With the passing of my beloved father it didn't matter where I lived.

In 1976 we sold everything (this would be the first of three times that I gave up all or most of my possessions) and left for the United States with our children who were then eight and six. We boarded the plane to America with only one suitcase each, a small amount of money and no job prospects. Talk about optimistic! Fortunately we were able to stay with my sister-in-law's parents in Dayton Ohio. Much to our children's delight, we found out that they owned a candy factory. The factory was every child's dream and could have been the basis for Willa Wonka and the Chocolate Factory. There were loads of chocolates, candy and taffy. The aroma was fabulous. There was also a small store in the front of the building where the customers would come to buy their treats.

After four months of searching my husband was offered a position with an American firm. The position required him to go to Toronto, Canada for six months to work in their Canadian office. After this we were to return to the United States. We arrived in Toronto on a cold, snowy, November day dressed in our Australian clothes – not at all appropriate for such a cold climate.

We soon became acclimated and applied ourselves to learning about our new home. We began appreciating the multicultural lifestyle in Canada and our new lives in Toronto. When the initial six-month assignment was completed we knew we had to make a choice. We felt very much at home in Toronto and wanted to stay in the city. The decision meant that my husband had to leave the American company. Fortunately he was soon offered another position with another transport company and we continued our life in Canada. There were times when I missed Australia, but I had great confidence in my husband and was prepared to support him in whatever he did. I took care of the home and children whilst he worked at his goal of becoming a millionaire.

After about four years of working with the new company my husband was given the opportunity to purchase a medium-size transportation company in Toronto. It had good assets with several hundred trailers and tractors and other well-maintained equipment, so my husband was able to convince the bank to lend him money to buy it. Four years later we sold it for several millions dollars to a much larger company. Was this luck or destiny? Certainly hard work was involved. I also now realize that my husband was practising the law of attraction without even knowing it.

My husband met his goal to be a millionaire by age forty. We lived the rich life with a home in the upscale Toronto neighbourhood of Forest Hill and one in Boca Raton Florida. We owned four cars: three Mercedes and a Porsche and flew first-class around the world. Yes we were the modern jet setters. I wore Ungaro clothes and the sky was the limit.

Many years later our prosperity would be a great lesson for both of us. We experienced acquiring great wealth and then (separately) losing it all.

Certainly one of my bigger lessons in this lifetime was to discover that money is not security. Money is just energy that can be used in both good and bad ways. Our materialistic society identifies with it far too much, but money itself is neither good nor bad it is the people behind it and how they use it.

It was interesting that when I was wealthy I was treated very differently from those with less. This was especially true of financial institutions. I was treated as someone to be cared about and respected and (it seemed) their staff would listen to everything I said. Things were markedly different once the money was gone. It seemed as if I quite suddenly didn't have a voice. Well, I suppose to them I didn't since money is the only language some people can hear. I always thought that by having lots of money I was protected and had security but now realise that the only true security one can have is within and it doesn't depend on a bank account.

Oops!

I had just purchased a beautiful, red Mercedes 560SL sports car and was driving on the highway with the hood down. It was a beautiful sunny day and my long, blond hair was flowing in the wind. I was thinking how great I must look as I pulled up at the liquor store to purchase some wine for dinner. When I stepped out of my car to cross the road it was if something pushed me and I went rolling down the road. My freshly cleaned white, linen suit was filthy. As I came to a stop it was as if someone said to me, "You think you are so great, take this." Lucky for me there were no cars on the road.

It was a good lesson because it wasn't the real me to be feeling so full of myself. I very sheepishly drove back home without the wine.

The Questioning Begins

One day whilst in a designer store in Florence, Italy with my wealthy friends I noticed how excited they were to buy the latest clothes. I felt like I didn't belong there. It seemed so artificial and boring. I suddenly felt that there had to be more to life. Every time I purchased an emerald (my favourite stone) I was very happy, but within a few weeks the happiness would disappear and I needed to buy more and more emeralds to fill the void. I know, it seems like such a trite problem, but I at least I realized that there was an emptiness that couldn't be filled with things.

Being wealthy is fine so long as it doesn't control you, but it's very difficult to not fall into the money trap of making more to spend more and "needing" to get ever more, and better stuff, and staying on the gerbil wheel all the while knowing it'll never be enough.

I was beginning to feel that my life was being wasted and there was something I needed to do but didn't know what it was. The fear of death at this point was becoming stronger as I had the feeling that if I died at this point my life would have been a waste. I kept asking myself if this really could be all there is to life.

I couldn't shake the unhappiness that had enveloped me. I travelled back to Australia for weeks at a time feeling that it would help, but it didn't. My husband couldn't understand me and felt that I had every material thing I could possibly need or want, and asked what was wrong with me. It was finally clear to me that what I wanted from life was not what my husband wanted.

We finally made the decision to separate and the marriage ended.

I knew that I needed to make a move and had no idea what was in store for me. I was about to go on a very tough spiritual journey that would last for twenty-five years and counting. I'd like to think that the toughest lessons are completed.

Within a few weeks of being alone unusual things started to happen. I had never thought about reincarnation or spiritual things. All I knew was what the nuns had taught me so I was a little astonished when I started seeing things. Interestingly though, I never worried about my sanity. I knew there was an explanation and I just had to trust that I would find it.

Shortly after the separation I was walking down my stairs when I found myself watching a scene that I had no doubt was from a past life. How was this possible and how come I just knew it as surely as I knew my name? It was like seeing a piece of a movie. There I was dancing with a handsome man somewhere in Austria around 1850.

I could see what I looked like. Surprisingly, the woman looked exactly as I do in this lifetime. I was wearing an exquisite pale blue gown which was swirling as I danced. My partner was wearing a white military uniform.

The couple was focused on each other with such intensity that I could almost hear music.

For several weeks after the vision I started to see more glimpses of the Austrian lifetime and then other lives as well. It was as if I opened up a side of me that I didn't know existed. I still don't understand why or how I had these visions, along with the many other experiences, I just know that none of it has been an accident and has propelled me to where I am today.

CHAPTER THREE

My Spiritual Journey Begins

Pushing Past Fear

I BECAME DESPERATE FOR HELP to get me through the divorce and seeing images from another time wasn't making things any easier. I felt like I had jumped into a river and was treading water and was afraid to move. The currant was pushing me forward and I had no choice but to start swimming as I couldn't return to my old life. The problem was that fear kept me from relaxing into the new direction of my life. I knew there was something that I was moving toward, but I was afraid to find out.

Now I understand that my path was meant to happen. I probably was even part of the planning before coming into this life. But back then I felt very alone and confused and even lost at times.

Seeing a previous life was only the beginning. I had a strange experience one day when I was babysitting a three-month-old infant. This child meant a great deal to me. I was lying on the bed looking into his clear eyes. There was a knowing as we both looked at each other and a voice inside of me said, "It's me." Immediately I just knew that this little one was the soul of my father. It hit me as a complete surprise. When I started to think about it I realized that this baby had the same birthday as my departed father who had been deceased for ten years.

One morning I was very upset about the thought of being alone for possibly the rest of my life. I was sitting on the edge of my bed praying to Jesus and asking for help. As with the child, I heard a voice inside of me. I was being told to look up. I ignored it as I thought I was imagining it, but again the voice said to look up .I still ignored it. Finally for the third time, and with more strength, it said to look up. I decided to look up and I was facing my mirror. The voice said, "Push back your hair." I had very long hair and it was hanging in front of my face. I did as instructed and looked into the mirror. Suddenly this hot feeling came over me and I began to shake. My face started to take on a transparent image of Jesus .I was in awe. Then the voice said, "You are my image and I love you. No harm will come to you if you continue to have faith and believe in me."

Then the image disappeared and I could see my own face again. This happened about twenty years ago and I recall it as clearly as if it happened today.

I immediately called my friend who is a Roman Catholic priest. I told him what had happened and asked him why Jesus would appear to me as I am just an ordinary housewife?

His reply was that it was ordinary people who were most likely to experience something like this, not rich or powerful ones.

Eventually these experiences and knowings helped me to find the courage to push through the wall to the other side, trembling and terrified as I did so. An amazing thing happened: I discovered that fear was an illusion and disappeared once I faced it. Remember that fear is what feeds the negative energies and we become their food source, so by facing your own fear you become free. If we face it and acknowledge it, fear can change into a higher vibration or simply leave us.

It took me four years to fully move out of the marriage because I was terrified to live alone. The fear was overwhelming because I never had taken care of myself. How would I manage? What would I do? Would I get through this transition? Eventually I realized that I am much stronger and resilient than anyone, including myself, had ever given me credit for; but back then, I was shaking in my boots as I made my first steps into my independent life. I wasn't just leaving the familiarity of my marriage, I left a circle of friends from that life as well.

Whenever I made drastic changes such as ending my marriage, moving from meditation and Indian teachings to learning chi kung, kung fu and Chinese philosophy I lost a lot of friends. When someone jumps out of the circle and stops acting and thinking the same as the group it forces the others to re-assess their own lives and they usually don't like the exercise. It's much easier to just gossip about someone else and is much more reassuring if everyone acts and thinks the same way. Accepting change, whether in our own lives or the lives of those around us can be a big leap of faith. It demands that we accept that our own thinking, or our group-thinking, isn't necessarily the best or only path to go down in life.

I feel that life is very simple yet complicated. The simplicity of life is to lead a loving, pure and compassionate existence and to care for our fellow human beings. The complicated part is our ignorance about the higher intelligence that appears to be orchestrating all of this. I also feel that we are accountable for everything we do here, both good and bad. When we see our life in front of us as we are about to leave this body we will experience all the bad we have done to people and all the good.

Some of us will not go back to our origin but instead will go into a layer waiting to reincarnate again. For myself I feel that I have been here for many lifetimes and would very much like to go back to the origin and not reincarnate.

Meditation

A few months after the separation I met an artist. He had a great calmness about him and enjoyed spending time alone. I admired is calmness and asked him how he managed it. He told me that he had been a meditator for ten years. From his description of his experiences it sounded like meditation could be the tool I was looking for to get me through the difficult post-marriage period.

At first I questioned having to pay so much to learn Transcendental Meditation, but I kept studying my friend and observed how calm he was.

I decided, what the heck, I would try it. It turned out to be one of the best and strangest things I ever did. I jumped into it whole-heartedly as it was giving me exactly what I needed. Looking back it was very inexpensive for what it gave me.

I began with forty minutes a day: twenty minutes meditation in the morning and twenty minutes at night. After some months I decided to further my meditation to a couple of hours per day by learning the siddhi program and becoming a yogic flyer.

Early into practising the meditation I would be woken up at night with words in my head and was compelled to write them down. This went on for approximately four weeks and each morning as I read what I had written it looked like a jumbled mess, but as I studied them they started to take shape. I feel that the resulting poems were given as a gift showing the simplicity of how we need to live. I've included them at the end of this book.

Everything was progressing well so I decided to go to the United States for an in-house course to get the final siddhi – the one for yogic flying. My flight home was uneventful and I was enjoying the new, expanded program.

I had been instructed to stay very quiet for the next few weeks as my nervous system would be very delicate from all the intense meditations. Unfortunately I didn't take heed of this advice and went immediately to a very loud disco the night after arriving back in the city. Within a few minutes of listening to the loud music I became disorientated and couldn't hear because of a loud gushing sound in my head. I returned home as quickly as I could. The next morning I had trouble standing up. It was as if I were on a ship on very rough seas. I managed to make my way to the hospital where I was told that the hearing in my left ear was almost completely gone. The doctors were very clear that I wouldn't be getting my hearing back in that ear. I was devastated and blamed the deep meditation but eventually resigned myself to coping. There is still a wind-gushing noise in the ear but I hardly notice it these days. I've gone to several specialists, both in Western and alternative medicine, but the original diagnosis was correct and nothing can be done about it. Thankfully I learned how to compensate for the hearing loss and my balance returned.

Shortly after this deafness I had a vision of a past life where I was doing something terrible to people. They were about to be killed and were begging for mercy. I ignored their pleas. I suspect that the past-life karma could be the reason for my permanent deafness. I'm grateful that it is only in one ear.

The hearing loss taught me to learn from negative experiences, including possible karma from past lives. It also forced me to go inward to get away from the very loud gushing sound in my head. I found that meditation brought relief and helped me to cope with the loss. I even experienced periods when I would forget about the sound and would hear it only when I thought about it. The loss definitely pushed me inwards where I started to discover the real me. The mind is so loud but the real essence of who we are, i.e., the soul, is very quiet and it requires attention, calmness and silence to hear it.

I practiced Transcendental Meditation for over ten years and during this time I had many visions but I never did levitate or even hop. I was repeatedly told that it would happen eventually, but it didn't in all the years that I practiced. I even went into the Catskill Mountains in New York State where I would meditate for most of the day for months at a time.

As a final effort to get back my hearing I decided to do puncha karma. This ancient healing process cleanses the body through many enemas, warm oil massages and meditation. The idea is to calm the body down with meditation so the healing can take place from the treatments.

One of the primary treatments is an Ayurveda massage with warm oil infused with special herbs. Two Ayurveda massage therapists work on you so that both sides of the body are massaged in co-ordination with each other. This is wonderful for relaxing the entire nervous system.

My favourite treatment was the dripping of warm oil back and forth across the forehead for twenty minutes. This treatment can put one into a deep euphoria.

Deepak Chopra was the lead doctor of the health centre at that time. I felt very confident about the facility as he is a man of great integrity who was just beginning to become the international sensation that he is today. The facility quickly began attracting patients from many walks of life. In fact at the time I was there one of the Beatles was also attending the clinic.

It was interesting that when I had my pulse read I was told that I had a digestive problem and I argued that my digestion was great as I rarely had pain or discomfort in my stomach. I was then told that a digestive problem manifests itself in the sinuses and around the eyes. Well that was exactly the problem I was having.

The treatments were definitely working because each time I returned home I would start to expel toxins. This is a slow process. We accumulate many different types of toxins throughout our lives, so we need to appreciate that it will take some time to reverse the process and start healing. As I said, nothing brought back the hearing, but I did get much healthier in the process.

It seems that many of us are so afraid to die that we listen only to Western medicine rather than giving natural therapies a chance. My theory is that our collective fear of death is perpetuated in order to keep us running to medical professionals when we are ill, rather than taking responsibility for our health by preventative means. We need to appreciate that the body is a gift and respect it, nourish it with good natural food, and get lots of rest. In return we can avoid many of the illnesses that plague us today.

Ask your body what it needs. I think you'll be surprised, once you learn how to quiet the mind and listen to something other than your own chattering ego. You will discover how intelligent the body is. For example, if you're in a supermarket and walking by the produce section take time to notice if you have a slight urge to purchase something such as an avocado. It could be the body telling you that it needs it for some nourishment at this time.

Provence

By now I had a healthy settlement from my divorce but the money didn't give me emotional security. In fact, one day I said to myself, "I have money but no deep happiness inside." The meditation was definitely helping with calming me but I felt empty and was still seeking something else. What, I didn't know.

I decided it was time to do something that would challenge me and give me strength to live alone while stretching my boundaries. France appealed to me so I enrolled in a school in Provence to study the language. I was asked to accompany another student who was also coming from Toronto. This woman turned out to be very difficult and rude. I spent two days with her in Paris waiting to take the train to Provence and quickly realized that I couldn't possibly spend the whole month with her. I won't go into the details. It is enough for you to know that she fits the description for narcissistic personality disorder.

On our way down to Avignon we stopped in Lyon for the night to wait for the next train. I was in such despair that I went for a walk and found a beautiful small church on top of a hill. I went inside and prayed for help. When we arrived in Avignon we were met at the train station by the teacher who was driving us to her village in the mountains. We were told that there was not enough room in the house to accommodate both of us so I was to stay at the house at night and the other student was directed to go down in the village to sleep in another house. I was so relieved that I (inwardly) gave thanks.

The next day this student borrowed a neighbour's dog and when asked to give him back she refused. The townspeople got very upset. Only three hundred people lived in the village and they all met for an emergency town meeting. They decided she must leave and told her to pack her bags, drove her to the train station and told her not to come back. I realised then that there was power in prayer and I again gave thanks. There is also power in the French not putting up with bad behaviour.

A Return to Spiritual Questions

Upon my return to Toronto I decided I needed more spiritual information so I decided to take a course on the gospels of Matthew, Mark, Luke and John at the University of Toronto. All the students in the class were studying to become either ministers or priests and I wondered what I was doing there. I didn't want to become a minister but I had a very strong thirst for knowledge about God so I forged ahead.

I learned that miracles (or most of them) did not happen overnight and in fact healing miracles sometimes took years to complete. It was also interesting to discover that the readings of Matthew, Mark, Luke and John all had their own interpretation of the Gospels, so one must wonder which one is correct. I have since learned that there were many other gospels, but they weren't included in official Christianity and have largely been lost. This makes it all the more important that we learn to trust ourselves and seek out knowledge from many areas.

In between studies I dipped back into the dating world. I was certain that I would meet another man and marry again since married life was all I knew. I had relationships, but none that were worthwhile. I realise now that re-marriage would have stopped, or at least slowed down, my spiritual growth. As painful as it was, I had to acknowledge that I was going to be alone. A permanent relationship would have drained my energy as I would have given up my power to my partner. The only way that this would not happen would be if I were to meet a man with the same energy as myself. If one has a higher energy than their partner the lower energy will absorb the higher energy and this can result in illness and fatigue, so it is important for both to have the same energy level.

I decided to sell my home and everything in it in order to speed up my transition into a new life. Even though my home held many beautiful memories of family I realised that I needed to make a clean sweep in order to create space to bring new things in. I knew that I couldn't simply hide in my home and wait for things to happen in my life. I had to take action and create space for the new energy to come in.

I employed a company to sell everything as I realised that if I tried to do this myself it would be too difficult. I walked away from my home with one suitcase. I would like to say it was easy to walk away from that life, but the truth is that I was shaking and terrified. It took a few months before I adjusted and I realized that I only walked away from possessions that can be replaced by new ones. The memories will always stay with me. This exercise taught me that one can let go of material things and survive.

This was the second time that I gave up all my possessions. Many years ago an astrologist told me the amount I was prepared to give up in this incarnation would determine on how far I would advance. I had no idea what she was talking about as it was before my spiritual awakening. Now I see how accurate she was as I have now, at the age of sixty-seven, given up all my wealth and hopefully a lot of my ego, but unfortunately not all of it. Trust me, this was not voluntary and it was a slow, painful road, but I am now a lot happier and more content than before. My feeling is that when we leave our body it will be a lot easier if we are not attached to anyone or anything. Perhaps this is why there are ghosts as they are not able to let go of everything and maybe don't even know that they are dead.

Being on my own gave me the time and the push to seek out tools to work on my soul development, pursue the purpose of my life, and be open to all that was being offered to me. I was beginning to understand that I wasn't alone and that there was a Creator, or God, or Source, or Tao, depending on what you want to call it. Quite frankly there isn't an adequate name for it, but our intellect requires a name. We also have a name whilst we are here in this body but when we leave we do not need a name.

We would look at life very differently knowing that death only happens to the body while our soul lives on. It is my feeling that when we die we exist as a vibration in another layer.

Of course not everyone believes that the soul lives on, but I strongly feel that everyone needs to have the opportunity to at least explore alternative health and belief systems. Unfortunately, often parents feel that their children are an extension of themselves, rather than fully separate beings with a separate path and aren't open to that exploration.

It continues to amaze me that we are not taught anything about life and death and transition in schools. We are taught math, history, science, and if we're lucky, some art, but not the most important thing about our existence. No one mentions spirituality or the soul in schools. Religion is taught in private schools, or the separate school system in some jurisdictions in Canada, but my experience is that this isn't as progressive as spiritual teaching needs to be.

It's as if someone or something wants to keep all of us in darkness. Maybe it is to keep us so busy that we won't pursue our birthright; which is to become enlightened. We are made to feel weird when we even ask questions about our existence before we incarnated. Of course not everyone believes that the soul lives on when we die, but we need to at least allow the discussion to occur.

It is not a religion, but a wisdom that we all need. In an ideal world spiritual knowledge would be the higher learning we pursued. A major part of a more enlightened curriculum would be an emphasis on the oneness that we all share. We need to know that whatever happens on the other side of the world, e.g., earthquakes, wars and tsunamis, has a direct effect on us, *now,* no matter where we are. Our middle axis is connected to the earth's middle axis and we are all part of source. We truly are all one. Whether we like it or not, we feel what others feel.

CHAPTER FOUR

An Active Lifestyle

A Fork in the Road

WHEN I WAS FIFTY-FIVE I was introduced to a healer who taught chi kung and kung fu and practiced healing techniques involving acupuncture, herbs and incense. He also worked with the elements of nature: earth, fire (sun), water, wood, and air.

He told me that I had the ability to heal people but first I needed to get stronger. When you do healings on people you can absorb negative energy from them and it is necessary to be strong so the healer isn't taken over by the patient's energy. Negative energy can be illness, anger or sadness (which is another form of anger). Interestingly he also told me that when you are healing people you can also heal yourself because you become a servant of God. It is possible to advance into a higher vibration by giving of yourself and thinking more of others while deciding how you can help them. Remember that we are all one, so whatever you do to others you also do to yourself.

My teacher suggested that I stop the long meditations as my body was getting weak and I needed to gain strength. At first I felt that he was wrong and that I still needed to meditate. Eventually I did stop the Transcendental Mediation program as I felt that he had something to teach me. I replaced it with intense physical training in chi kung and later kung fu. I progressed to practising up to five hours, six days a week. This schedule lasted for five years. At the same time I had healing sessions with my teacher and began to gain enough emotional and physical strength to ask my teacher about training to work with the elements.

I was told that I had to continue working on my own health before I could work effectively with the elements and help others. He said I had too much fire inside and needed to cool down. It was demanded of me to go into the cold river. This wouldn't have been my first choice as I didn't like swimming, let alone cold water. It was a crisp, October day the first time that I went into the Niagara River and stood chest-deep in the water for forty minutes. When I came out I was madly shivering and raced home to warm myself.

I had a strong fear of the water and was terrified to go under. One day my teacher told me that if I didn't conquer the fear I'd have problems with my kidneys and bladder as they are the water element organs. Naturally this made me more determined to get over my fear of water. Every morning for months I'd go down to the river and force myself to go under. At first it was only for a few seconds until I gradually built up to the point where the cold didn't bother me at all.

Now I can stay underwater for much longer periods. I've lost my fear of the water and can even say that I love it because of the energy and peacefulness I gain after a dip. When I come out of the lake an exhilarating feeling comes over me because I've pushed heat out of my system, which in turn makes my body light and relaxed. Too much heat causes bile in the liver which in turn spreads to other organs. In some cases too much heat can also cause cancer. The cold water is also amazing for the skin. It gives colour and smoothness to the skin because the blood is forced to the surface and increases circulation.

I've even gone into the Niagara River with ice floating on top. I simply pushed away the ice to get in. Mind you at this temperature I could only stay in for a few minutes and then go under just once.. Even today I go into the cold water of Lake Ontario very early in the mornings. To gain maximum energy from the water the best time to go in just before dawn and stay there as it becomes light because the energy is much stronger at that time.

A Return to Australia

In 2000 I took a break from my studies to return to Australia to see my mother. Earlier that year I had a desire to be with her when she passed. I was her only child and I wanted to prepare her for her passing. I prayed for assistance as to when I should go. Soon after, a date of November 10, 2000 came to me as the day that I needed to be in Australia.

About three months prior to the November date I received a call from my cousin to inform me that my mother was very ill with cancer and that I needed to come home immediately. She is a nurse and recognized the signs of my mother losing her battle with cancer. This was earlier than I had planned and became another lesson for me to listen to my own wisdom. In preparation for my departure I went to my teacher and asked for some special oils and incense to help with her passing. As I turned to leave he said, "If when you go to the plane and you do not feel to go at that moment, don't go."

I thought about what he said very seriously and decided to go with my inner feeling and called my cousin to inform her that I wouldn't be arriving until early November. She was very upset with me, and told me that my mother would not last that long, but I decided to go with my own timing rather than panicking and leaving immediately.

I arrived in Australia on November 3, rented a vehicle and began the drive to the nursing home to see her. Along the way I spotted a beautiful Buddhist temple and felt a very strong pull to take a closer look. I was not disappointed. The grounds were lush with hydrangeas, jasmine, lilies and wisteria. The tropical riot of colour was a welcome relief from the drab Toronto November that I'd left behind. Carefully placed fish ponds and cascading waterfalls added to the tranquil atmosphere. I felt very lucky that I happened to see it from the road and decided to see if they rented rooms to the public. My excitement turned to disappointment when I was told that they were fully booked. I told the monk that my mother was very ill and I needed a nearby place to stay while visiting her and asked if he could recommend a place that would have a good atmosphere. The monk then looked at me and said, "I will find you a room as I can see that you need it."

I hadn't realized how tense I'd become until I felt relief wash over me once I was assured of a place in this peaceful facility. All the rooms in the temple were bright and clean, but even more important, the atmosphere was calm and tranquil. It was indeed the perfect place for me to stay while I helped my mother in her final days.

After putting away my things I resumed my journey to my mother's nursing home. My first action upon seeing her was to put special oils on her body and burn incense in her room. This became a regular part of my daily visit. Now that I think about it I'm surprised at how easily my mother accepted my ministrations. It was certainly different from her regular routine. I'm also grateful that the nurses didn't stop me from burning the incense! This was a valuable time spent together with each other as we were never very close. She seemed in reasonably good spirits for a seventy-five-year-old cancer patient, but it was clear that she was declining. One day she told me that her body was getting weak and she thought that soon she would die.

At seven in the morning on November 10 I woke up thinking that this was the day of her passing. The phone rang and it was the nursing home telling me that my mother had been transferred to hospital because of haemorrhaging. I immediately went to see her. She definitely was weaker, yet somehow she recovered enough to go back to the nursing home after about ten days. I was assured that it would probably be okay for me to return to Canada. My cousin said that she would take over her care.

I had only been back in Canada for twenty-four hours when I received the call of her passing.

The night before my departure for Australia my teacher told me that my mother might not pass whilst I was there. I thought to myself that he was wrong and I was confident that I knew better. For whatever reason my mother didn't want to pass whilst I was with her. Thinking back on all of this, the date that I had of November 10 was actually the beginning of her passing as she passed on November 23, 2000. I am very grateful that I was able to spend time with her during her final days and I hope that it made her passing easier.

CHAPTER FIVE

Connecting the Dots

The Ego

MY RETURN TO CANADA ALSO meant the resumption of my training. I had asked to awaken (become enlightened) in this lifetime and spirit answered my request by throwing a lot of things in my face. My ego was being retrained and I must say that it was not a pleasant experience. It's necessary to heal the ego so that it becomes a healthy and integral part of your being rather an aspect of self that fights your attempts to awaken.

Another spiritual teacher I've come across, Inelia Benz, reminds us that, *"The ego is not something evil. The ego is not something we should fight, try to destroy or invalidate. . . Often we will deny our mistakes, will blame others, and will self-destruct due to the fear of loss. The ego fears loss of face, loss of wealth and even loss of its very existence. The ego will often stop a person from their personal ascension work because it fears that once the person ascends, there will be no more 'person,' no more 'self'. . . The ego is always a victim. A person run by the ego will always have something or somebody to blame for their unhappiness, their distress, suffering, and circumstances, which are never good."* From Spiritual Ascension 101, Spiritual Ascension Course by Inelia Ahumada Avila, Unit Eight, Healing the Ego.

Ego and survival can show up in many ways. Part of my path was to integrate my ego in a healthier way, including a journey into detachment from possessions, money and even people. I thought money was my security. I had a great deal of money and had feared losing it. This should have been my first clue because I now realise that when one has a great fear around something it's often an indicator there is a lesson to be learned. Of course now I see that money comes and goes. It is all part of the learning experience. It's a question of how one handles the changes as to how easy it will be to cope. See it as a lesson. See it as the illusion for which it is. We do not take it with us. The only thing we take is our soul and our experiences. Of course we don't all have to learn in the same way. There are as many paths as there are people. The loss of my material possessions was the path that I ended up on. It hasn't been easy, but I do feel that I've come a tremendously long way in my development.

There are three questions I asked myself regarding my soul development:

- How much love have I given in this lifetime?
- What have I done for mankind?
- How much have I learned about life – why am I here, what is my purpose, and what is creation?

I continually ask myself these questions as a way of gauging my growth. It has been helpful for me to take stock of myself so that I can see that I actually have progressed. Journaling is part of this process. It is a way to be gentle with ourselves and see how far we've come, or where we might want to do more work.

The Lord's Prayer

If we study the Lord's Prayer I feel that we can get to God, creation or source, whichever name you prefer to use, by ourselves. This prayer shows us how.

Our Father who art in heaven, hallowed be thy name. Thy kingdom come. Thy will be done on earth as it is in heaven. Give us this day our daily bread and forgive us our trespasses as we forgive those who trespass against us and lead us not into temptation but deliver us from evil. Amen.

My interpretation of the prayer is this: *Our Father who art in heaven -* heaven is inside of us and we produce our own heaven and hell and God also resides in us. We need to accept our own divinity. *Thy kingdom come* —is a knowing that we are part of creation and all will be well when we act in accord with our own divine nature rather than letting fear take over. *Thy will be done on earth as it is in heaven* – to live a wise, compassionate and peaceful life. *Give us our daily bread* – a prayer for our needs and to recognize when our needs are being met so that we can survive on earth. *Forgive us our trespasses as we forgive those who trespass against us* – we ask for forgiveness in ourselves as we also forgive those who wrong us. The final request is to, *deliver us from evil* – evil can be anger, anxiety, depression, and heat in our system.

It is us, not someone outside of us who can lift us out of our various malaises. At this time, more than at any other, we are to be our own teacher. The universe wants us to recognize ourselves for the divine beings that we are.

This life is a learning process and we are given many opportunities to learn from past experiences and past lives. The Chinese philosophy is that we should be very appreciative to experience difficult times as we are burning off our karma. We come into this life with a suitcase of karma. How we live our lives will determine how empty the suitcase will be when we leave. Most spiritual teachers will say that when we sincerely ask to grow into enlightenment we need to be prepared for many changes in our life and what could be seen as difficult times. This is so that we can burn through our karma in order to learn how to gain balance and not live in duality.

Distractions

We are distracted with very little real news and encouraged to remain a materialistic society, instead, we need to wake up so that we will know who we really are. Many of us are working several jobs just to survive because of inflated prices and our materialistic life style. The result is that we don't have time to stop and take time for ourselves. Could this be deliberate?

I was listening to a nightly radio programme in which a guest-speaker discussed how the elite don't have much compassion and seem indifferent to the suffering of the people. The question put to the guest was, "Did their children not have more of awareness about compassion when they were young?"

She answered that they were taken from their mothers as toddlers and put into the care of nannies and then boarding schools. Wow! That reminded me of a friend who is married to one of the elite. At one of their huge employee gatherings her husband made a comment that one of his employees reminded him of a dog. I was horrified and couldn't believe that he said that, even worse, he had said it in front of the employee and his fellow workers.

This man heads a huge European-based company that has existed for hundreds of years. I was told that as a child he was in the care of a nanny, put into a boarding school and often left there by himself on Christmas vacations. It is the making of Ebenezer Scrooge again and again. They don't learn how to have sympathy for the average human as they are kept in seclusion from them.

The Elements

Along my path I've learned how completely connected we are to nature.

My teacher taught me the relationship of our bodies with all the elements. When you think about it, how would we survive without air, sun, water, earth and trees? I know most people take all of this for granted and so did I.

My teacher moved my nature and health education to a northern Ontario forest where I started working with the elements and began appreciating how connected we are to nature. I didn't like going into the bush in Australia and hadn't become a hiker in Canada. But in my fifties I entered yet another phase and began climbing trees, carrying heavy loads in a large backpack, learning how to find my way in a forest, and testing my physical limits as they'd never been tested before.

Each time I thought I couldn't go on I was told that I was stronger than I realised.

He had me scootching upside-down along a rope strung across streams and rappelling down large boulders. Of course I had to climb back up and repeat the exercise, often doing this several times in a row. These exercises were part of my teacher's program to show me how the elements can strengthen and even heal the body. It worked.

One day I was instructed to climb up onto the roof of a small building and watch my teacher. He said that he would call the wind. I wasn't sure what he meant with such a statement and was amazed as a huge gust of wind blew over us as he did his calling.

He used a specific invocation to call the elements and taught it to me. I use the invocation when going into the water to enhance the healing experience.

Each of our organs is specifically connected to one of the elements.

- Air is connected to our lungs and large intestines.
- Sun is connected to our heart and small intestines.
- Water is connected to our kidneys and bladder.
- Earth is connected to our stomach and spleen.
- Wood is connected to our liver and gallbladder.

As we contaminate the elements we also contaminate ourselves. We are all part of the earth and are more connected than our standard teachings indicate.

Our bodies are approximately eighty-five percent water and we rely on all the elements to remain alive, so why would we not be part of all the elements? I realise now that I relate strongly to water and don't know why I was so afraid of it. Incidentally, my sign is in Pisces which is a water sign.

Invoking the Elements

I call upon the magnificent force of the element water.

I invoke you for your assistance in this moment of this cleansing

in the way to obtain the release of the negative forces and the

destruction of them and the liberation of the power of the creation.

How part of the power of the creation of the universe is living within me

light of light

brightness of brightness

origin of origin

size of size

mysteries of the life

brighten the mysteries

origin of the light

may I possess

I possess for the centuries of the centuries of the creation

So be it

This invocation can be done for all the elements. Simply replace water with earth, fire, wood or air as desired.

CHAPTER SIX

Changing Routines

Chicken Feed

I'VE LEARNED THAT CHANGING OUR lives and getting out of routines and a life of habit is important. It can be as simple as taking a different route to the store or going on a different walk. It's important to not just move through life following the same-old, same-old every day. So naturally the changes to my lifestyle kept on coming. I was becoming more practical and decided to raise chickens. My intention wasn't to become a chicken farmer. I just wanted to learn how to care for these creatures and enjoy my own fresh eggs and organic chicken meat. With the help of some friends I built a small pen

before ordering sixty baby chicks and two roosters. Luckily I had moved to a vineyard in Niagara-on-the-Lake and I had a very understanding landlord. I can imagine the reactions of my former city neighbours to a chicken coop!

It was a wonderful experience for me and I learned a lot about them. I had no idea how to raise poultry or how to

build a chicken coop. The closest I'd ever been to a farm was the coffee plantations in New Guinea nearly forty years ago. My tool bag for my big building project was an old designer handbag. Boy, did I get teased. It was a good thing that I had a friend who gave me advice regarding the chickens whenever I needed it. Most of what I learned though was simply by being on the job.

Some of the chickens would follow me around the vineyard where I was living at the time. They would even jump up on my lap for affection. Wow! I didn't know that chickens did that. As the chickens grew the two roosters became very protective.

One day I was making my usual trip to the chicken pen with their food when one of the roosters came running up to me as if to attack me. This rooster had grown very big and was quite strong. As he took an attack stand I said, "Don't you dare attack!" He clearly wasn't impressed and flew at me.

I jumped back and luckily had a stick in my hand. I wacked him on his head and he fell back, but immediately took a stand again with aggression in his eyes. I said again, "Do not do this." Clearly he wasn't listening to my stern tone. With lightning speed he flew for my face. I hit him so hard that he fell onto the ground, stunned for a few seconds, and got up and walked away. He never tried to attack me again. Of course I realised that he was protecting his hens and didn't see that I was simply coming to feed them. But the lesson I learned was to stand up to them and not show fear, otherwise I would be in the same situation again and again. It's a good lesson for dealing with any of the bullies we come across. They may have their reasons, but we still need to stand up for ourselves. I certainly don't advocate whacking people on the head with a stick though.

Not My Time

Summer moved into fall and the inevitable winter. The lessons continued for me, both directly from classes and sessions with my teacher, and through daily living. Sometimes I wondered if I really could keep up the pace, but I was too much in the thick of it to even think of backing out.

I noticed that lessons that spirit was throwing at me were becoming even more dramatic as I progressed.

I felt I must be making some progress and was even giving myself a pat on the back when my teacher suddenly told me to pack some clothes and drive up north to a property in the forest by myself and not leave the property until I was instructed to do so. I was there for three days before I was told that it was time to come back home. On the drive back I hit black ice on the highway and went into a spin. There was heavy traffic all around me and I lost control of the car. In the next minute I was sliding sideways and saw the wheels of a huge semi-trailer headed toward me. It looked like I'd be trapped under its carriage so I resigned myself that I was going to die. Suddenly my car stopped on the side of the highway facing the correct way. I have no idea how I ended up there. I realise now that my teacher had knowledge of a possible bad accident happening in those three days and sent me away to be safe.

I still don't know how I came out of that spin without having a fatal accident, but I'm thankful that I survived without injury and not even a scratch on my car.

When I arrived home I was still feeling pretty shaken up and just wanted to lie down. The phone rang. It was my son calling to tell me that he had an accident. It turned out it was at the same time that I spun out of control. Unfortunately his car was damaged but he was not injured. Could it be that he felt my terror as I was spinning out of control and he in turn lost control of his car?

Healing Work

Shortly after sliding across the highway my teacher told me that I was physically prepared to work with people using the techniques he'd taught me. I began with on-touch therapy which involves touching areas of the body that relate to different organs. The energy of the organ is enlivened and the body heals itself.

One of the most rewarding occupations is helping people. While working to heal people you help to heal yourself. It was very energising work and I loved doing it. The downside is that you can absorb negative energies, so it is very important to work on yourself after. I would do several cleansing techniques such as going into the cold water, or using oils and incense, and sometimes a combination of all of these. Another way is to go into nature to gain energy from the elements. For instance, find a tree that appeals to you, hug it, and take three deep breaths while holding it. Remember that trees are alive and have a very strong energy. Remember to offer thanks for this.

I needed to use many of my cleansing techniques when I worked on a friend of mine who was gravely ill. I'll call her Julie to protect her privacy. She had deep anger and was told by my teacher (who was also her teacher) that if she didn't change she would get sick. He reminded her that anger causes a lot of heat in the system and makes the liver hot, which in turn creates bile, which eventually spreads throughout the body. This can then turn into a cancer. Unfortunately Julie could not or would not find a way to deal with her anger and developed cancer. A lump grew in her breast and her skin started to ooze a sticky liquid.

She decided to follow her doctor's recommendation and underwent many intensive treatments of chemotherapy and radiation for several months. Finally she ended up in the intensive care section of a hospital, dying. The nurses informed the family that the medications were not working and that she would die very soon. A desperate relative of Julie's contacted my teacher who was away out of town. My teacher then called me and said that I should go to her with oils to administer touch therapy.

When I arrived at the hospital I took one look at her and knew that her circumstances were not exaggerated. I placed my hands on her abdomen and started to pray to creation to save her. As I did this Julie sat up, opened her eyes and became conscious that I was there. She hadn't been responsive for many days prior. When I touched her body she was so weak that I could hardly pick up her energy. I finished and went home feeling very sad for her. The next morning I received a call from my teacher to say that she was recovering and to go back and work on her again. When I arrived at the hospital I couldn't believe the difference. Her energy was a lot stronger and she was talking to me. After a few days she was feeling much better and was sent home.

My teacher told her that she had been given the gift of life, but if she continued with her anger she would get sick again and the next time it would not be possible to save her. Unfortunately she continued to hold on to her anger and suffered through more radiation and chemotherapy. Western medicine didn't work and she died a terrible death.

The treatment for cancer today is archaic with the use of poisonous chemo therapy and radiation. I recently heard about a doctor who completed autopsies on several hundreds of bodies. He stated that they didn't die from the cancer they had, but from the effects caused by chemo and radiation treatment. So why do the doctors today insist on this treatment? Why are we still so focused on treatments that do as much harm as good?

We all have cancer cells in our bodies; if the immune system is not strong, the cancer cells can take over. I know this is a radical statement. Is it possible that our weakened immune systems could be caused by genetically modified foods, contaminated air and contaminated water?

I also had the pleasure and relief of working with other, less serious ailments. The client was at her wits' end and she was adamant that she didn't want to go on hormone replacement therapy for menopause symptoms. She wasn't able to sleep and had lots of night sweats. She had tried many vitamins and herbs with little long-term success. I first started doing pressure points on her and then told her to prepare for a swim. It was fall and I arranged to pick her up the next day at six in the morning. When I went to my car there was frost on it and I was wondering how my client was going to react knowing that she was going into the Niagara River.

When I arrived she was shivering outside waiting for me and as she got into the car she took one look at me thinking that I must be crazy. We got to the river and I told her to go into the water but she hesitated so I insisted, and in she went. The water was very cold and after a few minutes I told her to go under. When you go into cold water the heat rises up to the head and it is necessary to go under to release all of it. She gritted her teeth and gave me a look that said, "This better work."

She then started to come out and I said to go under again, and then again for a total of three times. She completed the immersions, ran for her towel and jumped into my warm car. We repeated this for a few more times over the week that she was in town. She soon stopped her hot flashes and by the end of the week she announced that she was sleeping through the night and feeling better than she had in years. I told her to find some fresh water to swim in where she lived. If this wasn't possible I suggested cold showers – and I do mean cold – as a substitute. This simple treatment is free. It does, however, demand some will power and commitment to take charge of your well-being.

I used this simple cold-water treatment on another client. This woman was dealing with a lot of anxiety (which indicated that she had too much heat in her system). The reaction was immediate and positive so I suggested that it would be beneficial for her to go into the water each morning and stand there up to her chest for a period of time. The next morning, back at home in the United States, she found a perfect spot and proceeded into the lake. She was standing there quietly when police saw her and decided that she was suicidal. They dragged her out and humiliated her with questions as to why she was in the water and wouldn't believe her when she said she was in the water for health reasons.

The police honestly thought that they were saving her and wouldn't leave her in peace in the lake. If it had been in the middle of the day on a crowded beach things might have been different. Our society really is afraid of the unusual and the lone person being quiet. Or perhaps it is a reflection of the reliance most of us have on some "other" coming along to tell us what to do and save us from ourselves. Either way, we will need to become much more independent as we move into this changing world and start to open our awareness to a different lifestyle and to all possibilities. Know that there will be some raised eyebrows but go ahead and do it anyway.

In order to build up the immune system we need to eat natural food and food that is suitable for our body-type and needs. There are foods that will strengthen specific organs, just as other foods will weaken them.

For example, to strengthen the:

- liver and gallbladder eat green pepper
- lungs and large intestines eat garlic
- kidneys and bladder eat cilantro
- heart and small intestines eat red onion
- stomach and spleen eat tomatoes

These vegetables make a wonderful general-health soup when tossed in a pot with a whole chicken (bone-in for calcium), some cumin and pure sea salt. Your body needs salt for the immune system and nervous system, it just doesn't need quite as much as we put into it and it really is important that it be good-quality sea salt. If you want to stay healthy you must take control of what you put in your body. It's like a car: if you put in top quality oil and do oil changes regularly it will run much better.

It's also necessary to cleanse the body by pushing out old faeces stuck to the intestinal walls. They can seep back into the body causing illness. The cleansing can be done in many ways and you will need to consult a professional as to the best treatment.

Nature is very silent and has the power to heal so many problems. Water in particular is a powerful element that we can use much more effectively to maintain good health. In general, full-body immersion in cold water is an excellent remedy for health problems caused by anger. It is even more helpful to be in fresh water (rather than relying on a bathtub or shower). The energy from the fresh water will have a greater healing capacity. As

I've mentioned, cold water can push out heat that can cause anger, thus nipping health problems before they take root. I guarantee that you'll feel better after. Cold-water treatment is also beneficial for high blood pressure, liver and lung problems.

The earth is also an excellent way to expel heat from the system. Lie down on the earth, especially on moss, and breathe deeply. The earth will help heal the stomach and spleen and can be beneficial for symptoms like arthritis, which is caused by inflammation and heat in the system.

The most important thing to appreciate is the connection that we all have with creation, to see how all of nature is connected to us, and how we can heal ourselves through nature. On those mornings when I am swimming in the lake with the sun rising on the horizon, I wonder why I'm the only person taking advantage of this perfect place, enjoying this perfect moment.

The Powassan Property

Since I was having success working with the elements, specifically water, I decided that it was time to buy a property up north so that I could work in the forest and learn more about nature. I found a ninety-acre, virgin forest about ten minutes out of Powassan, a small town just south of North Bay with a population of approximately three thousand. The property also had a very large beaver pond with lots of animals nearby. Within hours of arriving I sighted deer, rabbits, beavers and moose.

It was quite isolated and I fell in love with the beauty of it. My offer was accepted and I began a huge learning curve. Keep in mind that I was a city girl and knew nothing about living in the forest. It had no running water, hydro or plumbing. There were just thousands of trees and lots of wildlife. After my first week at the property I set out to return to my home in Niagara-on-the-Lake when I sighted a huge moose blocking my exit. I decided to turn off the car and look at it till it ran away. The moose was only about fifty feet from me and we stared at each other. I finally realised after fifteen minutes that one of us needed to move and I guess it would have to be me since the moose was standing his ground and not budging. I managed to scotch around it and drove off.

My first task as an acreage owner was to find someone to help me develop the property so that I could live on it. I was fortunate to find a local fellow named Roger, who was able to clear some land for me in order to put on two old school portables that I had purchased. My plan was to stay in one portable and use the other one for friends or health clients. Roger began the work of clearing one-hundred feet of trees for my portables and suggested that I needed a water supply. I replied for him not to worry because I planned on bringing up bottled water. He very gently said that it would be a lot easier for me to have running water. I just filed it under, "someday."

Roger was a very interesting person. He grew up in the bush, spoke with a slow calm tone and was clearly comfortable with country life. It was also very clear to him that I was still, very much, a city girl. One day as I exited the car I automatically locked it. He slowly said, "Yes! Only the city folk would lock their cars here."

He was right of course.

I trusted his knowledge about the area and realised that his advice was well worth taking. I was also getting tired of hauling up water from the city when I knew pristine water had to be on the land. I asked him to look for the water. He started digging eight-foot holes all over the property. Finally, after many attempts, he told me that he couldn't find water. I was now concerned as I realised that this could be a problem.

I'd been taught how to invoke the elements so I decided to put my training with the elements to use. I began scanning the property as I invoked the water element. Suddenly my eyes stopped in one spot. Immediately I felt that water was there. I called Roger and told him where to dig. I could see by the look he gave me that he thought I must be crazy. He responded that it was not a good spot. He then went into the forest and found a willow tree and cut off a Y- shaped branch to do some dowsing (an ancient practice used to find water). The dowser needs to hold the forked end of the branch while making sure that his palms are turned upwards.

As Roger was walking back with the branch it started to tremble and dipped down indicating a potential spot. He commented that there could be water there but he was standing in the middle of the road so it wasn't practical. I then asked for the stick. I went to the spot that I chose and immediately it started to tremble. Roger looked at me in disbelief but had no choice but to dig there. Roger went to work with the tractor while I projected for water. When he got down about eight feet he hit a huge boulder. This was to be expected as the property is on top of the Canadian Shield. As the boulder started to break up the water bubbled through.

He was very quiet and I could tell that he was trying to figure all this out. He then told me that I needed to wait for three days to see how much water was in the hole. After that he'd be able to tell if the well would draw a sufficient amount depending on the amount that collected. Each day I would check it. On the third day there was enough water for my well. The water was fabulous as it was filled with minerals from the rocks. I felt privileged and gave thanks to creation for this wonderful gift.

The next step was to build an outhouse as I was getting tired of going into the forest. I was sure that the animals would be happier as well. I decided on a four-foot-by-four-foot building. It was time to visit the supply centre back in Niagara-on-the-Lake to ask them what was needed for my project. They sold me the necessary materials and I drafted my son and two grandsons, Daniel and Nicholas, to help partially build it before transporting it up to the property. I didn't have any hydro so the rest would be completed by hand.

Completion was very challenging, but somehow I managed to get it up and completed with the help of my friend, Audrey. When we decided we were finished we discovered that the door wouldn't close because it was too wide. We needed to make the frame larger and I only had a hand saw.

Well, it isn't easy to cut a ready-made frame with a hand-saw. The frame had many curves in it but we finally managed to close the door.

When Roger came by to see how I was doing I was happy to show him that we had built an outhouse. I was very proud of our accomplishment and waited for his approval. He stood there quietly surveying the crooked door frame then very politely asked if there were any carpentry schools in Niagara. When he left Audrey and I promptly drove to the local store and purchased a strip of wood and nailed it over the crooked frame. Presto, we had a straight door frame. I'm relatively certain that the structure will not fall down on anyone.

I learned a great deal while working on this property and getting in touch with the forest. I remember my teacher telling me that you can do anything that you want if you put your mind to it. Yes, I understand that our society requires credentials for certain professions, but this was about learning how to be self-sufficient. I've certainly found that I'm far more capable than I ever gave myself credit for.

Instant Karma

I was fortunate to have a small lake nearby where I could continue my sunrise dips in fresh, cold water. Early one morning I was standing in the lake up to my chest and enjoying the powerful sunrise energy when suddenly a muskrat propelled itself up from the water and came face-to-face with me. I got such a shock that I screamed and the poor muskrat dived under the water. He never joined me again for a swim. I guess he was curious to see who was this crazy person standing there in his lake so early in the morning.

The animals didn't always run away, although they were certainly curious and some were quite happy that this city person had brought some new buildings for them to chew on. When all was quiet at night I could hear a porcupine eating away at the front door of my portable. Apparently he liked the wood that was under the door frame. I was getting concerned that soon I wouldn't have a door. A neighbour suggested that I put out some dry concrete with salt in it. The porcupine is attracted to the salt and eats the mixture. The concrete hardens in the animal's system to bring about a very slow and painful death.

This is a typical example of how I tend to listen to some people without thinking of the real consequences. I was so concerned about my door that I didn't give a thought about what this would do to the porcupine. I mixed up some concrete and salt and placed it at the door. As I was climbing up the steps of the portable I tripped and fell with great force onto my leg and hit my shin bone on the sharp, metal frame. I ended up cutting myself right through to the bone and was in agony. I climbed onto my bed while holding onto my leg. Immediately I could hear a voice saying, "Take that for the horrible thing you are about to do to that poor animal."

I realised that I was betraying nature and was very regretful that I even contemplated such a thing. I immediately went outside and took away the concrete. My leg became infected and I suffered for quite some time after. It was a painful lesson for me but would have been much more painful for the poor porcupine.

Chapter Seven

Life after Training

Become As Little Children

IT WAS A BEAUTIFUL FULL, harvest moon when I took a friend with me to Lake Ontario. As we stood in the cool sparkling water we could see the brilliant red glow of the morning sun peeking out over the horizon. The sky was filled with vibrant pinks and blues. Behind us was a magnificent full moon. The exhilaration of the cool water and its freshness had such an innocent feel about it that it reminded me of what Jesus once said, "Until we become as little children we will not enter the kingdom of heaven."

My interpretation of the quote is that when we see the full beauty of nature and experience it as innocent beings we will know what pure happiness is. Heaven and hell exist here on earth. It isn't a matter of waiting until we die. It is here now. We can make our own heaven or our own hell. The past doesn't exist, only the present. So it is important to live in the moment.

I have come to realise that creation speaks to us through other people. I had arrived at the point where I could no longer afford to stay in the wonderful farmhouse I was renting. All my money was gone. I won't go into the details other than to say that most of it was used for the cost of the training, studies and the expenses from improving the property up north. I needed to find a place to live in that would be comfortable and considerably cheaper than the vineyard that I had grown so very fond of.

I found a two-room apartment about one hour away. I prayed to creation and asked to be shown if it was the right decision. I was nervous because I was going from a large, three-bedroom house in the country to a tiny apartment in the city. The next day I received a phone call from a young friend who told me that she was having lunch with someone who happened to be reading some tarot cards for her. The reader informed my friend that she knew an older woman who was about to make a major move and to tell her that everything would go well because it would be very good for her. Since I was the only older friend who was about to make a move it seemed pretty clear that the information was for me.

As it turned out it was a good move. As soon as I signed the lease for my current apartment I sold the property up north. The sale enabled me to get out of debt and life became much less stressful. I knew that I was feeling considerable strain from my financial situation, but I hadn't realized just how much the constant worry was taking from me until the source of my worry was taken away. I feel that, despite the considerable pressure I was under, I probably dealt with the situation far better than I would have prior to my spiritual journey. Of course, some might say that the situation wouldn't have come up then. But I believe that the money would have been gone from my life one way or another. I am grateful to the wonderful network of friends who helped me ride out the situation. I'm also grateful that I was never particularly attached to my old lifestyle.

So for the third time I sold almost everything I owned. It has become increasingly easy for me to let go of things and not be attached to them. It is far too easy to become slaves to our possessions. My path has shown me that it is far easier to accept change rather than fight it.

Now that my life has become less complicated I can look back and realise that I have been very lucky to have had so many opportunities offered to me: some were very difficult and some were amazing. Through it all I continually ask myself, "What have I learned on this journey?" The answers keep me on track and I can see that the journey has been well worth it.

The Soul's Transition

I am currently living in a seniors building. The apartment I was offered was flanked by women who were very ill and dying. I was not aware of this and only found out after I moved in. Actually, I only learned about the illness of one woman. I often find myself around dying people. Perhaps this is a commitment that I agreed on before I came here to in some way assist with their exit.

The first woman died about one year after my arrival. As I mentioned, I was aware that she was very ill. I spent a small amount of time talking to her and made one of my special soups for her. The woman on the other side of my apartment was also dying. Unfortunately I didn't know this and didn't get to know her at all.

About two months after the passing of the first woman I started to feel anxious but couldn't understand why as there was no reason for it. Life seemed fine and I didn't have any worries, yet I knew that something was wrong and wondered if a family member was dying as it was a feeling I've had when this was about to happen. I couldn't find anyone I knew who was very ill, even so, a few days later I had a huge panic attack. I went outside to my balcony to try to calm down. As I come back into the apartment I heard lots of commotion outside my door and saw paramedics running past my apartment. About ten minutes later the panic attack stopped and I felt fine. I learned the next morning that the woman in the apartment beside me died at exactly the same time that I was having the panic attack.

I feel that the soul tries to attach itself to someone who they feel can help them. I meditate each morning and have a very calm atmosphere in my apartment. As she was leaving her body she may have tried to communicate with me. No doubt she was terrified whilst all this was happening to her.

For a few days later I was still feeling some anxiety. The soul can stay in this layer for up to nine days and it seemed that she was still around and possibly confused. One way to help a departed soul is to place three candles in a triangle with a picture of the departed person inside the triangle on the right and a glass of water on the left. Change the water each day and keep the candles burning for nine days after the passing. This will assist the departed and also help the person grieving. Make certain that the candles are on a fire proof container. Once you set this up it is important to continue it for nine days, otherwise do not do it.

The death seemed to be affecting me more than other deaths that I'd been around. I tried burning incense, meditating and going for long walks, but couldn't get rid of the anxiety which was starting to cause heat in my system. I had no choice but to follow my own advice and immerse my body in cold water to push out the excess heat and any negative energy surrounding me. It was a cool, mid-November day and off I went with some hesitation to Lake Ontario. The water was frigid. I took a deep breath and walked into the lake without giving myself too much time to think about it.

Unfortunately it was very shallow so I had to walk out about thirty feet to get to my chest. Luckily the sun was out and there was very little wind and no waves. I walked quickly and hoped to get into deeper water soon as my feet were getting very cold. Finally I reached the spot I wanted and quickly dipped in up to my chest. Wow! It was like ice and I still needed to go under the water to release the heat in my head. I immediately went under and jumped up in shock and quickly came out of the water, dried myself and put on some warm clothes. Of course this is something that I used to do regularly; nevertheless, it was a shock.

After the cold water dip I started to feel much lighter and cooler. The anxiety disappeared and a more relaxed and happy feeling came over me.

Gratitude

Each morning as I meditate and pray to creation, I am thankful for all the lessons and opportunities, both positive and negative that I've had and remember that this life is a gift I also give thanks for the abundance in my life of food, clothing, and love of friends and family. One of the biggest lessons that I have learned in this lifetime is to let go of the past and see everything as part of a contract that we agreed to before we were born. There are very few true accidents in life. It is important to know that and live in the moment.

I urge everyone to make their own commitment to find their path and move toward enlightenment. Mother earth is going through her own changes and we are going to be facing many challenges simply because we are part of her, so we will also have many challenges in the coming years. We will all need methods to deal with the emotions that will bubble up as we progress. Of course there will be some people who will refuse to change and grow. They like things just the way they are. They will face their own unique challenges and will have to make their own choices.

CHAPTER EIGHT

Food for Health and Healing

How to Cook

YOU DON'T NEED TO BE a Cordon Bleu chef to eat well. In fact, how you eat is almost as important as what you eat. It is very important to eat in a happy quiet environment and to offer up thanks for the food you are about to ingest. Remember that food has energy and giving thanks will help with digestion and absorption.

As a cook it's also important to feel happy and have good intentions for the people that you may be cooking for. Don't cook if you are angry as you'll make the food toxic for those who eat it. They won't understand why they feel bad after eating, but you will.

Also whilst cooking say a small prayer to creation to make the food nourishing and healing for the people who'll eat with you, or if you're alone say the prayer for yourself.

One of my favourite soups is a simple vegetable-chicken mix that helps all the organs of the body. I haven't included the amounts needed as it's important that you taste the soup as you're preparing it and add more of the ingredients as you see fit. So start with one of each vegetable and go from there. Your individual taste is what will make the soup beneficial because you are unique in knowing what your body needs. You'll know what you need through taste. You can add other vegetable as desired, e.g. carrots and celery.

CHICKEN SOUP

Ingredients

- red onion
- green pepper (capsicum)
- garlic
- tomato
- cilantro
- cumin
- sea salt
- chicken with bones left in
- chicken stock*

See the Food and Organs chart for a correlation of item and area impacted.

Method

1. Half-fill a large saucepan with water and add salt to taste. Bring water to a boil.
2. Add the chicken and some chicken stock and cook until chicken is tender.
3. Take out chicken and place on a plate to cool.
4. Cut up vegetables and put into broth and cook until tender.
5. If you want to add other vegetables, e.g., carrots or celery, do so now.
6. Cut up chicken into small pieces (discard bones) and place into the soup.

*You can also cook some marrow bones in the soup and eat the jelly-like substance inside the bone on bread with salt and lemon. This is very beneficial for your bones and blood.

GARLIC SOUP

Ingredients

- 6 large garlic heads divided: 4 for baking and 2 to fry
- 2 red onions
- 4 mushrooms
- 2 cups chicken broth
- thyme
- butter
- cream at end to taste

Method

1. Cut off the top section of 4 garlic heads, pour some olive oil and salt on top, wrap in foil and roast in medium oven until soft. Squeeze out the garlic once roasted and set aside.
2. Peel and separate the 2 garlic heads.
3. Peel and cut 2 red onions into 8 pieces.
4. In a large frying pan place a large chunk of butter and sauté onions and thyme till soft.
5. Add both raw and the squeezed pulp from the baked garlic heads and chicken broth to the pan. Cook on medium heat for about 20 minutes.
6. Add sliced mushrooms, salt to taste and cook for another 10 minutes.
7. Pour ingredients into a blender and mix until smooth. Add cream as desired.

NOTE: Garlic is an antibiotic for the body and especially for the lungs. It helps to heal pain and inflammations, purifies the blood and extracts negative gases.

Food and Organs Chart

ITEM	AREA IMPACTED
• red onion	• heart and small intestines
• green pepper (capsicum)	• liver and gallbladder
• garlic	• lungs and large intestine
• tomato	• stomach and spleen
• cilantro	• kidneys and bladder
• cumin	• eliminating negative energies
• Sea salt	• for the nervous and immune systems
• chicken with bones left in	• protein and calcium
• chicken stock	

CHAPTER NINE

Poems

Ten Poems

I AM INCLUDING THESE SMALL poems because even though they are childlike they have powerful messages in them. Although I wrote these, I feel that they are not from me but through me from creation. The first one was written to describe my love for the saint who I felt gained much insight into life and who resonated with me, St Theresa of Avila. She prayed for assistance to write because she disliked writing. I'm grateful that she wrote anyway.

St Theresa of Avila

St. Theresa, I would say
Loved Jesus in a special way

He showered her with love and courage
And gave her strength
To enter marriage

She fused with God
And God with her

Oh! What a sight to behold
the beauty of such a soul

Wisdom

When it comes to being wise
Look up to the heavens and rise

I love you God
I love you God
With such ferocity, how could I not be wise?

Just You and I

When we meet
Just you and I
Up to the heavens
We shall fly.
Together locked
In our embrace,
Seeking wisdom
At Heaven's gate

Compassion

In this world
Full of wants and desires,
Compassion is the key
For all you require

Loving and caring,
Is what we should share
In abundance today
It is much too rare

Immortality

Our love is deep
Our love is strong
Until we meet
The journey is long

We seek the diamond
We seek the gem

We won't give up
Until the end

Who is God?

Does God really exist?
How can He cause so much pain and suffering?
If He loves so deeply,
How can he allow all this to happen?

You are God.
You caused all this to happen.
You are an image of God.
The choices are yours.

Going Within

How to find light
In all this darkness

Go within

How to find God
In all this confusion

Go within

Open up your heart and soul
Bare it for all to see

See what you don't like to see
Have faith
To believe in God

Divinity

Oh! To be so divine
For the gods to be mine

I only hope and pray
That one day
They well choose
To set me free

Freedom

I love my freedom
It is so

I don't know why
But I just know

What is free?

What is free?

My soul is free
When ego is not me

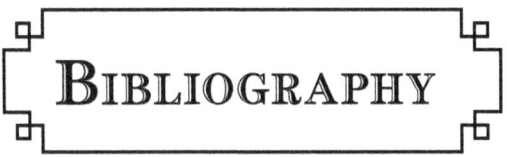

BIBLIOGRAPHY

— Inelia Benz: http://ascension101.com/

Robyn Ford is an artist, teacher and seeker. She has
practiced transcendental meditation and Chinese
healing techniques for the past twenty years.

Her passion for nature and the elements has
enhanced her abilities to help many people.

"Once we begin to really look around us and notice our world
we can begin to appreciate the wonder of life and our planet".

At 68 she still swims in the cold waters of Lake Ontario at sunrise.

Originally from Australia she now lives in the picturesque
town of Burlington, Ontario, Canada.

www.ingramcontent.com/pod-product-compliance
Lightning Source LLC
Chambersburg PA
CBHW020352290526
45785CB00005B/2241